Meandering

CHA

(1) Brampford Speke   3.5 miles

(2) Uffculme   3 miles

(3) Crediton via Salmonhatch   3 miles

(4) Grand Western Canal at Burlescombe   3 miles

(5) Shobrooke Mill   3 miles

(6) Lapford   3.5 miles

(7) Newton St Cyres   4.5 miles

(8) Tiverton   3.5 miles

(9) Bickleigh   4 miles

(10) Silverton   4 miles

DISCLAIMER

The contents of the Kindle e Book are correct at time of publication. However we cannot be held responsible for any errors or omissions or changes in details or for any consequences of any reliance on the information provided. We have tried to be accurate in the book, but things can change and would be grateful if readers advise us of any inaccuracies they may encounter.

We have taken every care to ensure the walks are safe and achievable by walkers with a reasonable level of fitness. But with outdoor activities there is always a degree of risk involved and the publisher accepts no responsibility for any injury caused to readers while following these walks.

SAFETY FIRST

All the walks have been covered to ensure minimum risk to walkers that follow the routes.

Always be particularly careful if crossing main roads, but remember traffic can also be dangerous even on minor country lanes.

If in the country and around farms be careful of farm machinery and livestock (take care to put dog on lead) and observe the **Country Code**.

Also ensure you wear suitable clothing and footwear, I would advise wearing walking boots which protect from wet feet and add extra ankle support over uneven terrain.

There are a few rules that should be observed if walking alone advise somebody were you are walking and approximate time you will return. Allow plenty of time for the walk especially if it is further and or more difficult than you have walked before. Whatever the distance make sure you have enough daylight hours to complete the walk safely. When walking along a country road always walk on the right to face oncoming traffic, the only exception is on a blind bend were you cross to the left to have a clear view and can be seen from both directions.

If bad weather should come in making visibility difficult, do not panic just try to remember any features along route and get out the map to pinpoint the area but be sure before you move off, that you are moving in the right direction.

Unfortunately accidents can still happen even on the easiest of walks, if this is the case make sure the person in trouble is safe before seeking help. If carrying a mobile phone dial 999 or 112 European Union emergency number will connect you to any network to get you help.

Unmapped walks we recommend that you take the relevant Ordnance Survey map and compass with you, even if you have a Smartphone, digi-walker or G.P.S all of which can fail on route.

Introduction

Mid Devon lies between Dartmoor, Exmoor and the Blackdown Hills. There are 3 rivers that flow through the district and they are the River Exe, the River Culm and the River Yeo. Raddon Top (770 ft.) is the highest point off the Raddon Hills, and in the early 90's excavations took place at the summit to reveal traces of an Early Iron Age settlement.

Meandering in Mid Devon is a quiet tranquil experience wandering through quiet country lanes, open fields, beautiful secluded bridle ways, green lanes and pretty canal towpaths. There are also the River Exe and River Creedy also adding to the beauty and cultural experience with some of the best wildlife in Devon. The Exe Valley is very quiet with the River Exe winding its way down the valley, with the neat tapestry of well-manicured fields on both sides of the river, this region down through the valley is arable land growing all types of crops. The River Exe features a lot in some of these walks with its twist and turns down from Exmoor it offers an immense variation of flora and fauna as it quietly flows through peaceful villages and busy market towns into the cathedral city of Exeter.

On some of the walks there are also woodlands which add to the excitement of a well-crafted walk, then on through the odd green lane which has been in place for century's with ancient man walking from village to town with their livestock to sale at the markets. Some of these walks are near to mills which many years ago were the heart of the village or hamlet, they brought wealth to these areas and help the nearby smallholdings also make a living.

Mid Devon is a well hidden jewel in the crown not as popular as other areas in Devon but criss crossed with footpaths and rivers and with the odd canal. The aim of the book is to introduce people to a different and stunning part of the Devon country side. The walks are ten of varied distance from 3 miles to 5 miles for all ages and fitness, the shorter walks can also be for families and with care and respecting the country code also for the family dog.

There are historical places nearby some of these walks, picturesque villages and ancient canals built to help prevent the trade ships from sailing around the Cornish Coast. All routes have full descriptions (always be safe and take a OS map 114 Exeter and the Exe Valley which is the complete area) the map is numbered with each section and distance of walk stated at start. The grid reference is provided and the local information of parking, bus service and trains if in area. There are cafes and toilets mentioned if in the area or on route.

If there is any outstanding places of interest I have mention this in the text along with related stories of the area or advised to check out the view from the top of a hill or along a riverbank.

Please remember if you have a dog to follow the Country Code keep on a lead in the lambing season and also when the birds are nesting especially around ground nesting birds to prevent birds deserting there nest and leaving the chicks to predators.

Please make sure you follow the Countryside Code, gates are normally shut by the farmers to keep farm animals in, but sometimes they may be left open so the animals can reach food or water. So be sure to leave gates as you find them or follow instructions on signs.

If you think a sign is illegal or misleading such as a PRIVATE or NO ENTRY on a public footpath then contact the local authority.

When out and about always be sure to use gates, gaps or stiles in the field boundaries if possible because climbing over walls, hedges and fences can damage them and increase the risk of farm animals escaping.

Be careful not to disturb ruins and historic sites because our heritage is for the future.

The dog is man's best friend and is very important to a lot of us, but they too have rules. Remember to ensure dogs do not disturb wildlife, farm animals, horses or even other people keep them under effective control.

There can be special dog rules which apply in particular situations, dogs maybe banned from certain areas that people use.

The access rights that normally apply to open country know as Open Access Land require dogs to be kept on a short lead between 1st March and 31st July to help protect ground nesting birds and all year round near farm animals.

If however cattle or horses chase you and your dog it is safer to let your dog off the lead. The dog will be much safer if you let it run away from a farm animal in these circumstances and so will you.

Dog mess is unpleasant and it can cause infections, so always clean up after your dog and get rid of the mess responsibly. Make sure your dog is wormed regularly to protect it, other animals and people.

BEWARE Ticks give you Lyme disease a bacterial infection that can be passed to humans through this small blood sucking insect. Ticks can be found commonly in woodland, grassland and heathland, both here and abroad. For symptoms check the Natural England website.

Meandering in Mid Devon

Chapter 1 **Brampford Speke**

Park & Start Grid ref; SX 926985

Distance; 3.5 miles

Level; Easy

Terrain; The walk is level through open meadows and patchwork of arable farmland. The path also snakes quietly along the ever twisting River Exe cutting its way through the beautiful Exe Valley. There can be some muddy sections so walking boots would be advised, to help with ankle support on some uneven ground

Refreshments; The Lazy Toad pub, and only on Mondays the Exe Valley Tea Shop

Access to start;
Go from Exeter out on to the A377 Crediton, then just after Cowley Bridge take a right turn to Brampford Speke just before the Bernaville Nurseries.
Bus Service only available to Bernaville Nurseries it is then a 2 mile walk to Brampford Speke.

The Walk

(A1)

The walk starts in the centre of Brampford Speke near to the church and the little primary school. Once at the school walk towards the fork in the paths and take the left hand path and drop down a slope and head to a bridge over the river.

After crossing the bridge go through the gate and take the path to the right, keep over to the left on the path near a fence and away from the river. This path avoids the soft mud on the lower path, continue along over a footbridge and follow the path around to a gate at the entrance to a small copse. Follow the path through the wood to a kissing gate go through and admire the view of the river from this high point once the old railway track into Brampford Speke. Carry along the track to another gate go through and continue through the fields along the path to the end finally reaching a lane on the outskirts of Stoke Canon.

(B1)

At the lane turn left and follow the lane away from the railway level crossing past a farm on the left and farm buildings on the right, then after about 500 metres there is a turning on the left ignore this and continue on down the lane to reach another turning to the left at a road junction which is about 1 mile. Take this turning to the left and follow the lane for just under a mile to reach a large barn on the right, then just a few 100 metres past the barn there is a turn to the right marked Exe Valley Way ignore this and stay on the lane, at the bend veer around to the left. Continue to follow the lane to the next bend and again keep around to the left, continue on through the lane with its twists and turns and finally reach a bend to the left, with a gate on the right.

(C1)

Go through the gate and follow the track down to the river. Then with the river on the right follow the riverbank back through the fields, go through a large gateway still following the river, cross a stile and through another field to reach a double kissing gates go through into anther field. Continue on through the field to reach a path through the hedge with a open space with a bench, then on to a stile cross over and into a field. Follow the path all around the edge near the river to finally reach a large metal gate. Once through the gate follow the path back to the small bridge near the start and then retrace your steps back to the car.

Local Info;

On the Brampford Speke walk you will see water meadows and the Ox-Bow lakes created by the river. Along the River Exe are many herons which are majestic birds growing up to 36 inches and often just standing absolutely still like statues. Also look out for the rare sighting of the otter, there are kingfishers, sand martins, egrets and mink.

This is a quaint piece of the Devonshire country side which is just north of Exeter. It is truly a magnificent area with its tapestry like fields woven to the blue sky and a touch of dark undulating woods all right on the edge of the Exe Valley.

The little village of Brampford Speke is full of thatched and cob cottages which is situated resting gently on a cliff of red sandstone just overhanging the twisting River Exe. The River Exe as changed its course over the years in this particular area which forms a common flood plain feature, this comes about with its strong flow and currents it cuts away into the outer banks. But this then will leave deposits of silt and debris along the inner bank were the current is not so strong. The result is that the river cuts across the bend creating a new course, this then leaves behind a curved ox-bow lake separate from the river. Also in this area are great trails like the Exe Valley Way and the Devon Heartland Way.

Places Nearby;

Exeter City the regional capital of Devon is only 5 miles away from Brampford Speke with its ancient Roman history and sections of the old Isca fort that surrounded the city. There are underground passageways and the new Royal Albert Museum which is one of the leading museums in the country. The 2000 year heritage is on show with the great Gothic St Peter's Cathedral and all this can be seen with a free guided tour from the red coats. Next to the Cathedral is the Mol's shop opposite the Royal Clarence Hotel the shop was once Francis Drake's coffee house where he meet Raleigh, Grenville and other seafarers, and at the opposite corner is the Ship Inn were all the medieval sailors met to swap stories of the high seas.

The historic Exeter Quayside is also nearby which gives plenty of scope to walk, cycle or even go by boat to enjoy the River Exe or the Exeter Ship Canal.

Chapter 2   Uffculme

Park & Start Grid ref; ST 062121 Coldharbour Mill car park

Distance; 3 miles

Level; Moderate

Terrain; The walk is mostly on the level with one steep climb near the beginning, then through open fields and gentle stroll along the riverbank. Beware there some muddy sections, so strongly recommend walking boots which also give support over uneven ground.

Refreshments; Coldharbour Mill and Mill shop.

Access to start;

Take the M5 and exit at junction 27, then at roundabout take third exit on to A38, then at next roundabout take second exit on to B3181 and follow signs to Uffculme.
Bus Service may be limited so check Traveline 0871 200 22 33.

The Walk

(A2)

The walk starts from Coldharbour Mill car park, go out the gate and turn right along the country lane. Follow the narrow lane over the bridge crossing the River Culm and continue on up the hill. Take the first road junction off to the left and stay on the lane until the road starts to veer away to the left, then at this junction take the lane to the right.

(B2)
Keep on the lane right to the end passing Gaddon House on the right and finally reaching a dead end for vehicles were the lane changes to Stoney Lane a narrow pedestrian lane which can be very muddy at certain times of the year. Stoney Lane then starts to rise quite steeply but once at the top what great views back out over the Culm Valley.

(C2)
The small track then bears round to the left just on the edge of Gaddon Wood. Continue to the top and look out for a signpost marked footpath on the left. Turn left in-between two banks and follow the track straight down to reach another wooded area known as Slow Jack. Once on the edge of the wood there are many signs and footpaths in all directions but continue straight on down what is known locally as Drift Road. The road then splits into two take the left fork and just a few metres further on take another left fork down a short but steep slope leading up to a stile.

(D2)
Cross over the stile and drop down the field keeping over to the right before reaching another stile. Go over the stile and continue down the field in the direction of a large metal gate. Once through the gate this brings out on to a lane turn left and continue to the end which is about a half a mile to a road junction. Cross the road with care and almost straight in front is a lane taking you back into Uffculme stay on the footpath to reach a bridge over the River Culm, cross the road and just before the start of the bridge turn left through a gateway between two walls down the steps to the riverbank.

(E2)
Follow the River Culm for about a mile through several fields to finally reach a kissing gate and an exit out onto a lane. At this point turn right and retrace your steps back to the car park at Coldharbour Mill.

Local info;

Coldharbour Mill as been a spinning mill for over 200 years, it is a rare example of surviving Georgian architecture. The Mill reopened in 1982 were it continued to produce quality worsted knitting yarn on its period machinery.

Places Nearby;

Hemyock Castle is set in the beautiful Culm Valley near to the quiet Blackdown Hills. The Castle is most likely built on an Old Roman Site which may have been a Romano British Farm or even a Roman Stronghold.

Chapter 3   Crediton via Salmonhatch

Park & Start Grid ref; SX 839995 near Crediton rail station car park

Distance; 2.5 miles

Level; Easy

Terrain; The walk as one steep climb and then levels out before dropping down into the valley for a beautiful walk back along the River Creedy.

Refreshments; The Railway Station Cafe

Access to start;
Travel along the A377 towards Crediton and on entering the outskirts of the town take the first left turn marked Fordton, do not cross railway crossing but take first left and park near station.
Bus Services is quite frequent to Crediton from Exeter, there is also a train service but check availability with Traveline 0871 200 22 33.

The Walk

(A3)
The walk starts at the little car park next to Crediton Railway Station, then with the station on your left walk to the end of the road to a junction facing the Dartmoor Railway Inn and turn left. Follow the road a few metres towards the railway level crossing and turn right just before the crossing. Once in the narrow lane turn right almost immediately and go past a car garage on the left and as the lane starts to rise keep and eye open for an hidden path on the left. Once locating the path climb gently to were the path widens and take the narrow path off to the left. Follow path to the end to meet a stile set back in the hedge, cross stile into field and follow the defined path up steep hill heading diagonally to the top right hand corner to a small gate. After going through the gate follow path through next field to reach another gate.

(B3)
Go through gate which leads on to a tarmac path, go past houses on the right were the path then splits into two, keep over to the left and go through a gate. Just continue on path to reach yet another gate go through and follow path to the end to reach a lane.

(C3)
Turn left at the lane and carry on down the lane keeping over to the right to enter a track that runs parallel with the lane. Keep on the track for a half mile to the end with house on the left and a garage straight in front. Go between the house and the garage keeping over to the left to go through a gate into a field. Once in the field keep over to the left and head downhill towards a small gate in the bottom left of the field. Go through gate and walk diagonally across to the right to another gate in the right hand corner of the field.

(D3)
Once through the gate turn immediately to the left and follow the tractor ruts through a large open gateway into another field. Continue to follow the tractor tracks to the edge of a steep slope then just when the track veers away to the left you continue on down the slope to a gate in the bottom right corner. After going through the gate turn left and follow the lane over the railway level crossing and past a few cottages on the left, then look out for a stone wall with a public footpath sign at the end pointing to the left. At this point there is a stile cross over into a field and follow the well-defined path in the direction of the river. Continue on path to reach a metal gate which leads into a large open field keep over to the left alongside the hedge to a gate next to the River Yeo.

(E3)
Go through the gate and follow the twisting path through a small wooded area to reach a gate alongside the riverbank. This gateway leads into a field follow the path keeping over to the left nearest to the hedge continue to the end to another gate. Once through the gate turn left and follow the narrow path to the end to reach a gate to cross the railway level crossing (**at this point take extreme care STOP LOOK AND LISTEN before crossing).** Once on the opposite side turn right onto the lane and follow the lane to the end, then at the road junction turn left to retrace steps back to the Railway Station.

Local info;

Salmonhatch is situated on the outskirts of Crediton, were the Church of the Holy Cross stands and the name Crediton are both inextricably linked with St Boniface. In 719AD Pope Gregory II commissioned (St Boniface) born in Crediton as Wynfrith in 680AD to a Saxon family. The Church of the Holy Cross as along and varied history dating back over a 1,000 years.

Places Nearby;

Crediton Railway Station was open in 1851 by Isambard Kingdom Brunel, the line today is currently the Tarka and Dartmoor lines which run parallel until Coleford Junction. This line continues to Barnstaple were you can walk the Tarka Trail to Bideford.

Chapter 4 — Grand Western Canal at Burlescombe

Park & Start Grid ref; ST 069170

Distance; 3, 5 Miles

Level; Easy

Terrain; Grand Western Canal towpath through beautiful country side through twisting country lanes and small villages.

Refreshments; Ayshford Arms

Access to start;
On M5 exit at junction 27, at roundabout take third exit on to A38 and then at next roundabout take first exit and then follow sign post into Burlescombe.
Bus Service very limited trains only to Tiverton check Traveline 0871 200 22 33.

The Walk

(A4)
The walk starts at Fossend Bridge Burlescombe on a rough parking area adjacent to the bridge, from the parking area exit on to lane and cross over bridge to the other side turn right down slope to the opposite towpath turn right under bridge and follow towpath to Fenacre Bridge. At the bridge continue straight on the towpath for about another mile to reach Whipcott Bridge continue past the bridge still on the towpath too Waytown Tunnel.

(B4)
Once at the tunnel climb the gentle slope to exit out on to the lane, turn left and continue to follow lane has it twists and turns all the way into Holcombe Rogus. On entering the outskirts of the village there is a small restored chapel on the right next to a road junction, at this point keep over to the left and follow lane round the corner towards the centre of the village. Ahead is the Post Office on the left and a lane just before the shop, turn left down lane go past the Prince of Wales pub on left continue to follow track on through the farmyard. Just at the end of the track is an open gateway with farm buildings on the left, continue to stay on the track as it narrows and follow all the way down to the end.

(C4)
At the end of the track the pathway splits into two, but keep straight on to a large metal gate with a yellow way-marker hidden in the hedge, go through the gate and follow the enclosed path to the left to finally reach a stile. Crossover the stile and follow the footpath over a bridge across a small stream this then reaches a large metal gate next to a stile. Once over the stile follow the path across a narrow footbridge to reach the final stile.

(D4)
After crossing the stile this leads out on to a lane, turn left which crosses Fenacre Bridge back down on to the Grand Western Canal towpath, turn right and retrace your steps back to Fossend Bridge.

Local info;

One of the main features in Burlescombe is St Mary's Church built in the 15th century which is in the reign of Henry VII. Ayshford Chapel is nearby in the parish of Burlescombe it is a 15th century grade I listed building now looked after by Friends of the Friendless Churches, this is just south of Ayshford Court and north of the Grand Western Canal.

Places Nearby;

Holcombe Rogus as a manor house know as Holcombe Court which was built by the Bluett family, this has been described as the best Tudor house in Devon.

Chapter 5   Shobrooke Mill

Park & Start Grid ref; SX 880990 on the lane near to the Beer Engine Pub

Distance; 5 miles

Level; Easy

Terrain; The walk as one steep climb early in the walk but mostly quiet country lanes and open fields with a criss cross of bridleways.

Refreshments; Beer Engine Pub in Sweetham

Access to start;
Travel along A377 to Newton St Cyres then just past the Crown and Sceptre turn right down lane marked Sweetham and Station and park on road near the pub. Bus Service only to Newton St Cyres must walk down lane to Sweetham.

The Walk

(A5)
The walk starts near to the pub the Beer Engine, this then follows the lane towards Crediton for about a mile before reaching a road junction. At the road junction turn left and almost immediately turn right and start to climb the long but gradual winding hill all the way to the top. Once at the top ignore the footpath off to the left and continue down the hill for about 200 metres to a sharp left hand bend. Then right on the bend take the bridleway straight in front and follow path through a wooded cover, this then opens up and the path goes to the left over a small wooden bridge on to a gateway.

(B5)
Once through the gate follow through the field keeping to the edge, swing around the field still with the hedge on right and start to climb up a slight hill with a view of St Swithin's Church Shobrooke in the distance. Continue up the path heading in the direction of the church.

(C5)
At the end of the field follow the track around to the left to reach the lane, then turn left and follow the lane around to the church, with the church on the right turn left and follow the lane back down the slight slope. Continue to follow the lane for about a mile before reaching a new metal gate and a kissing gate on right, go through the gate and follow well defined footpath across field to reach gate which leads out to a lane. Turn left on lane and follow all the way back down to the road junction, then turn left along road to reach a lane down to the right sign posted Newton St Cyres take lane and retrace your steps back to the start of the walk.

Local info;

Shobrooke is very much an agricultural area set just 2 miles outside Crediton and 6 miles from the regional capital of Devon Exeter City. In the area is the magnificent Shobrooke Park, there is however limited walking access in the park from the 1st October 2012.

Places Nearby;

Crediton is the nearest town with its many cafes and pubs, also the very fine Church of the Holy Cross with a history that goes back over 1100 years. In 910 AD Eadwulf of Crediton built a cathedral in the area, this was then later on moved to Exeter by Leofric.

Chapter 6   Lapford

Park & Start Grid ref; SS 732083

Distance; 4 Miles

Level; Easy

Terrain; The walk is mostly on the level with a steep climb in the beginning but it is necessary to wear walking boots it can be very muddy on some sections.

Refreshments; The Old Malt Scoop Inn

Access to start;
Follow A377 from Exeter to Copplestone on to enter Lapford turn right into village, continue up hill to reach car park on left in centre of village.
Bus Service limited check Traveline 0871 200 22 33.

The Walk

(A6)
The walk starts at Lapford village car park, exit car park turn left and walk up the hill. Up the hill there are two 16th century magnificent old cottages on left and opposite is what once the Old Lapford Steam Bakery, at this point turn right into Park Road following road around to the right to join Park Meadow Close, then at the top end of the close turn left and head for the stile set in the hedge. After crossing the stile follow the path in a diagonal direction across the field to reach a stile, then follow the path on to another stile at the top of the hill. Then drop down the hill to a stile in the bottom right hand corner, once over the stile go out on to a lane follow around to the right, then take the gravel driveway off to the left this is just left of Parsonage Farm. Keep straight on to a large gate next to two cottages on the right go through gate past farm buildings on right and finally up a slope to a farm gate.
(B6)
Once through the gate head diagonally climbing up the hill through the field to the

top right corner to a large metal gate. Go through the gate and head to stile on the right which leads into the next field. Keep over to the left and follow the hedge around the field to meet a stile in the middle of the hedgerow, cross the stile and go straight ahead to another stile. After crossing stile this leads out into a lane near Great Hole Farm and its out buildings then just a few metres to the left go through a small gate next to a large gate and cattle grid on to a driveway. Follow the drive to the bottom and follow the sign marked detour this will lead around the ponds and finally reach a gate. Go through the gate and rise up a gentle slope to a metal gate on the right, once through this gate continue down the track to the bottom to a stile cross over the stile and through the woods (may be a muddy section) go left to pick-up a track which leads up to a gate.

(C6)
Once through gate on to lane turn right and go past Filleigh Cottage on right and head towards Filleigh Farm at the farm the road veers to the left but take the farm entrance on right and follow the lane through the farm yard, go through the gate at the end of the farm yard on to a track and follow to a gate at the end. Go through this gate and immediately turn right to a stile, cross stile turn left and follow the grass track down through a gateway were the track narrows down to a enclosed footpath, follow to the bottom finally reaching a gate. Once through the gate turn right and follow the quiet country lane for about 1 mile back to a crossroad.

(D6)
Finally at the crossroad go straight across and follow the lane back into Lapford to retrace your steps back to the car park.

Local info;

This area of Lapford is known as the River Country mainly because there are many rivers nearby including the magnificent River Yeo.

Places Nearby;

Okehampton Castle is nearby along with the lively town of Okehampton, including the Museum of Dartmoor Life.

Chapter 7 — Newton St Cyres

Park & Start Grid ref; SX 880987

Distance; 5 miles

Level; Easy

Terrain; This is a gentle walk mostly flat level ground through farmland and along the River Creedy for a short distance.

Refreshments; Beer Engine pub

Access to start;

Travel into Newton St Cyres via the A377 in the centre of the village turn right marked Sweetham and Beer Engine Pub, then just after stone bridge over the River Creedy Park near the football pitch.
Bus Service only to centre of Newton St Cyres 1 mile to walk to start off route.

The Walk

(A7)

The walk starts at the Newton St Cyres Sports Field car park near to the rail station. Turn left out of the car park and follow the road towards the bridge over the River Creedy, then just before the bridge there is a public footpath sign pointing to the left, follow this along the River Creedy bank. Continue to follow the river for about 1 mile taking you through four fields before going through a gate with a footbridge to the right over the river at this point turn left away from the river. This goes over some rough terrain before reaching the railway crossing after about 400 metres **(Extreme care must be taken at the rail crossing)**, go straight through the field on the opposite side following the well-defined path to a small footbridge over a stream.

(B7)

Then go through two gates at each end of a small paddock, then finally following the pathway for about 400 metres to reach the road in Langford. Turn left at this point and after 100 metres turn right up Bidwell Lane a track alongside Langford House, stay on the track for 0.5 miles then at the top were the track turns left go right through a large gate, then almost immediately turn left up a slight slope and through a small gate set back in the hedge into the field.

(C7)

Once in the field there is a very clear path straight through the centre, then at the end of field do not go through gate but take a sharp left turn and follow the footpath that goes down the hill with the hedge on your right. Continue to follow the sometimes over grown pathway past Bidwell Barton on your left to finally reach the Upton Pyne to Shute Road.

(D7)

Turn left on the road and continue on past the Upton Pyne Equestrian Centre following the road straight ahead to Jackmoor Cross. Just a few metres past the cross over a stone bridge look for public footpath sign to the left, take the path and follow the brook for just under 500 metres. The brook veers to the left, but keep over to the right were there is no hedge and start to walk up a slope before rejoining the hedge on your left continue to follow to the top of the field to a large and small gates next to each other and go through gate out on to a road.

(E7)

Turn left on the road and then almost immediately right at Winscott Cross follow the sign into Winscott. Continue along the road past Winscott Barton Farm and further on past Norton Farm, then just past farm and up slope turn left past bungalow set back of road and follow lane to come into the little hamlet of Sweetham after about 1.5 miles stay on road through the hamlet to reach a road junction. Turn left at station road over the railway bridge until you arrive back at the sports field.

Local info;

The church of St Cyr and Julitta is a magnificent little church set up on a hillside just off the main road (A377) Exeter to Crediton road. The tower dates back to the 12th century and the clock was added in 1711 and inside an eight bell peal was included in 1733.

The wildlife is quite extensive with rabbits, squirrels, kingfishers, fish and frogs. Further out of Newton St Cyres there are foxes, deer and wild boar, but please take the necessary care not to disturb the boar and always to be safe keep your dog on a lead.

Chapter 8   Tiverton

Park & Start Grid ref; SS 96312366

Distance; 4 miles

Level; Easy

Terrain; Grand Western Canal towpath via town and countryside, then back to the canal basin along the disused Tiverton railway line.

Refreshments; Grand Western Canal Basin cafe and food

Access to start;
Follow the M5 to junction 27, follow through on A361 into Tiverton and then follow sign markings for canal basin.
Bus Service is limited check Traveline 0871 200 22 33.

The Walk

(A8)

The walk starts at the canal basin car park, go up on to the towpath and follow in an easterly direction past new houses on the left before disappearing into the country surrounded by wildlife. On the way to Tidcombe Bridge a half mile along the towpath look out to the left to catch a glimpse of Knighthayes Court once owned by John Heathcoat-Amory the grandson of the inventor John Heathcoat.

(B8)

The walk continues form Tidcombe Bridge following the natural twist of the old canal to go under Warnicombe Bridge and winds past Snake Wood to finally after just over a mile reach Manley Bridge a round arch stone bridge. Go under the bridge and then immediately turn left up the slope and off the towpath into a small car park exit out onto the road and turn right. Follow the road for about 200 metres and just on the left past the old railway bridge turn left down the narrow path marked cycle route 3.

(C8)

This path takes you down to the disused railway track covered with trees and bushes which is full of magnificent wildlife. If you stay on the rail track it brings you into the outskirts of Tiverton, there are a few footpaths on the left that you can leave the railway track and go back on the canal towpath. Once you have come to the end of the disused railway track you exit a gate on to a path next to Old Road then after about 100 metres turn left into Lewis Avenue at the road junction keep straight ahead into Hermes Avenue continue up road to top right corner and follow the narrow pathway back to the canal basin and car park.

Local info;

The name Tiverton is derived from Twy-ford-ton or Twyverton meaning the town on two fords. The town is at the confluence of the River Exe and River Lowman, with occupation going back to the Stone Age times. There was also an Iron Age Fort and Cranmore Castle that stands at the top of Exeter Hill. Then there was a Roman Fort which was discovered on the hillside below Knighthayes Court near Bolham. In the centre of the town is Tiverton Castle first built in 1106 as a Motte and Bailey which was extensively remodeled in the 13th and 14th centuries?

Places Nearby;

Barnstable is thought to be the oldest borough in England which dates back to the 900s. It was the medieval period that made Barnstable important with its import and export of merchandise making it a thriving trade centre. In 1588 Barnstable help to defeat the Spanish Armada by sending five ships manned by Barnstaple men. The Barnstaple past is still present today with great guided heritage trails through the town.

Then there is the great walk along the Tarka Trail which can be joined at Barnstaple railway station heading out to west to Bideford on this popular traffic free pathway. This gives you great views of the Taw Estuary, reaching Fremington Quay along the way which also forms part of the South West Coast Path.

Chapter 9   Bickleigh

Park & Start Grid ref;   SS 5938969

Distance; 5 miles

Level; Moderate

Terrain; There are country lanes, with one steep climb there are some muddy tracks so walking boots for comfort and to overcome uneven ground. The area around is farmland and steeply wooded hillsides.

Refreshments; Bickleigh Mill and the Trout Inn or the Fisherman's Cot.

Access to start;

Travel along the A396 from Exeter which will take you to Bickleigh just before the Fisherman's Cot and the stone bridge over the River Exe.
Bus Service is from Exeter to Tiverton check Traveline 0871 200 22 33.

The Walk

(A9)

The walk starts at the public car park next to Bickleigh Mill, go out of the car park under the bridge to the A396 road and turn right and with great care cross the bridge on the main road near the Fisherman's Cot. Once over the bridge turn left onto the A3072 and follow the brown signs marked Bickleigh Castle. Take the first lane off to the left following the Exe Valley Way past Bickleigh Castle on the right continuing for about half mile past Way Farm on right and then New Barn also on right before taking a right turn on the next lane marked with a sign in the hedge Lee Cross and Perry Farm.

(B9)

This is a narrow lane which can be busy with traffic from local farms, follow the lane for nearly a mile as it climbs steeply uphill which passes by Lee Farm on the left. Continue straight ahead along the lane to pass Perry Farm start climbing before reaching a sharp right hand bend with a green lane off to the left.

(C9)

Take the green lane on the left and continue to follow all the way to the top, once near the top there is a converted church with a sign that is marked St Martin on left ignore the pathway to the left at this point and continue to climb up the hill. Then just at the top the lane begins to drop down and after 50 metres reaches a tarmac lane.

(D9)

Turn left at the lane which is part of the Exe Valley Way down a steep hill, there are magnificent views from up here in all directions across the River Exe and Exe Valley. Continue to follow the lane past the Trey Mill Farm on the right straight along the lane. Just by the mill there is a public footpath that takes you down by the River Exe and across a suspension bridge on towards the disused railway track on the left but this is privately owned and there is no public right of way. The pathway does continue straight across the field to reach the A369 main road and you can turn left and follow the road before turning right into Bickleigh village and back to the public car park. N.B. I would strongly recommend not to take this route in the interest of safety and you return to Trey Mill Farm and retrace your steps back along the quieter route to Bickleigh Mill.

Local info;

Bickleigh lies in the valley of the River Exe were it meets the much smaller River Dart. Just outside Bickleigh is a beautiful medieval stone bridge across the River Exe, near the Fisherman's Cot. The bridge gave rise to the rumor that Paul Simon was inspired to write the Song Bridge over Trouble Water although he did stay at the pub sadly this is not true.

Places Nearby;

Bickleigh Castle which was formerly known as Bickleigh Court is a fortified manor house, The castle was once much larger a Norman Motte of the late 11th century which was dismantled in the mid-12th century comprises of many buildings from various periods, in Norman times a Norman Chapel and a baptismal font were added which is now used for weddings, now it is believed that there has been a chapel on the site since the 6th century on the foundations of an old Saxon building.

Bickleigh Mill was built in the 18th century and continue to work until 1960 when it was devastated by floods, it is now the Devonshire Centre with crafts and working farm and the mill.

Also alongside the mill is the Devon Railway Centre the original site of Bickleigh Station built by South Devon Railway in 1885. The site was taken over in 1997 and restored laying down narrow gauge track.

Yearlstone Vineyard in 2008 was named England's fastest improving vineyard, and with its perfect position sat high above the River Exe as turned Yearlstone into a much visit destination.

Chapter 10   Silverton

Park & Start Grid ref; SS 95604 02841

Distance; 4 miles

Level; Moderate

Terrain; This is a great walk there is however one long and steep climb for about 1.5 miles but the lanes are quiet and then the open fields at the top with magnificent views all around.

Refreshments; Lamb Inn

Access to start;
At Cowley Bridge out of Exeter follow the A396 through Rewe and Stoke Canon before seeing sign post on right to Silverton.
Bus Service limited check Traveline 0871 200 22 33.

The Walk

(A10)

The walk starts off in the centre of Silverton at The Square at the heart of the old village from there carry on up Fore Street go past the Post Office and just follow the road right through the village ignoring all the turnings on the way.

(B10)

Once on the edge of the village the road starts to climb in the direction of Butterleigh which is then about 1.5 miles just up and up but the views are spectacular the further up you rise. On the way up the hill you pass Aish Farm and old 17th century building and further on Land Farm which is the home of Silverton's own Barron Brewery. After reaching the top of the hill Christ Cross the road to Butterleigh veers around to the left, but at this point take the lane that goes off to the right and follows a flat level road along what appears to be a ridge.

(C10)

Then after almost a mile further on there is a green lane off to the right be careful not to miss it, at the point where the road starts to rise. Follow the track (this can be muddy at certain times of the season) all the way down to the bottom to reach Greenslinch Farm. At the bottom follow the lane around to the right and go past Greenslinch Barton were the track widens and go straight ahead past cottages on your left to follow a narrow footpath 500 metres to reach a stile with a public footpath sign. Take the footpath to the right, ignore the path up across the field, once on the path follow the hedge line down to the bottom right corner and cross over the stile, go down track for 50 metres to reach the lane.

(D10)

Turn left at lane then just 50 metres along lane with a well mark footpath turn right at first gateway, cross the stile and head up hill in a diagonal direction to follow the top hedge line and follow down to the right hand corner to a small gate. Go through the gate and straight through the small paddock to another gate. Once through the gate follow the fenced in path around the primary school to exit on to Coach Road, turn right and follow road up towards Prispen Close turn left just before the close between Prispen Fields and the houses on left to follow a narrow footpath on into Parsonage Lane bringing you out at the crossroads of High Street and Fore Street, turn left and retrace your steps back to the village square.

Local info;

Silverton is a large village and also one of the oldest villages in Devon which dates from the first years of Saxon occupation. The main feature of the village is the old oak tree which is over 1000 years old. The village is situated between the River Exe and River Culm, and walking up Fore Street with its leat of ever flowing water you will see thatched cottages with the cob walls and also late medieval buildings.

Places Nearby;

Killerton House is well worth a visit built in the 18th century then owed by the Acland family one of Devon's oldest families but now in the hands of the National Trust. One of the masterpieces of Killerton is the garden created by John Veitch with its rare trees and beautiful rolling Devon hills.

Printed in Great Britain
by Amazon